TOTALLY PACIFIC NORTHWEST!

Peg Connery-Boyd

sourcebooks
jabberwocky

Hawk's Nest
Publishing, LLC

KEEP PORTLAND WEIRD

Copyright © 2016 Hawk's Nest Publishing, LLC
Cover and internal design © 2016 by Sourcebooks, Inc.
Illustrations by Natalie Thomson
Cover design by The Book Designers
Internal design by Travis Hasenour/Sourcebooks
Cover and internal images © shutterstock/Evan Meyer, shutterstock/Dave Newman,
shutterstock/Jess Kraft, shutterstock/dovla982, shutterstock/Perutskyi Petro, shutterstock/
Alex Helin, shutterstock/Hank Shiffman, shutterstock/Denise Lett, Thinkstock/stock_shoppe

Published by Sourcebooks Jabberwocky, an imprint of Sourcebooks, Inc.
P.O. Box 4410, Naperville, Illinois 60567-4410
(630) 961-3900
Fax: (630) 961-2168
www.sourcebooks.com

Source of production: Versa Press, East Peoria, Illinois, USA
Date of production: April 2016
Run number: 5006374

Printed and bound in the United States of America.
VP 10 9 8 7 6 5 4 3 2 1

WELCOME TO THE
PACIFIC
NORTHWEST

LET'S COLOR!

TOTALLY PACIFIC NORTHWEST!
A TOTAL SECRET!

Use the key to decode the message.

C L I M B

E V E R Y

M O U N T A I N

KEY

= A	= E	= M	= R	= V
= B	= I	= N	= T	= Y
= C	= L	= O	= U	

Solution is on page 51.

LET'S SOLVE!

Help the salmon swim back up the river.

START
HERE!

Solution is on page 51.

TOTALLY SCRAMBLED!

Unscramble the letters of these animals found on the coast of the **PNW**!

MLSONA

__ __ __ __ __ __

CRAO

__ __ __ __

BCAR

__ __ __ __

SLEA

__ __ __ __

AHKSR

__ __ __ __ __

YERG AHWEL

__ __ __ __ __ __ __ __ __

Solution is on page 52.

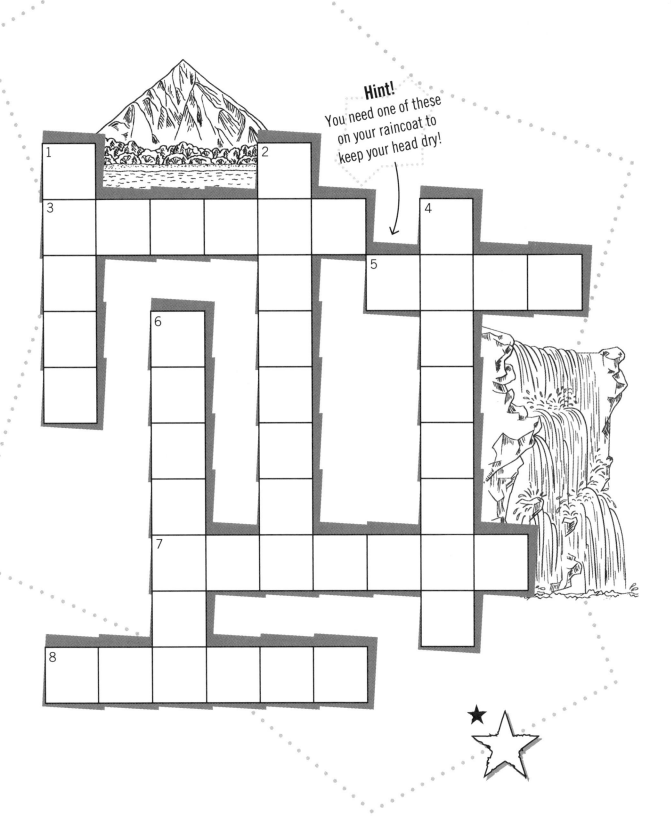

Hint!
You need one of these
on your raincoat to
keep your head dry!

KEEP PORTLAND WEIRD

PACIFIC OCEAN

CRATER LAKE

BEND

SALEM

OLYMPIA

PORTLAND

SEATTLE

WALLA WALLA

MT. RAINIER

Choose a **PNW** city or landmark from the word bank and write it on the corresponding line.

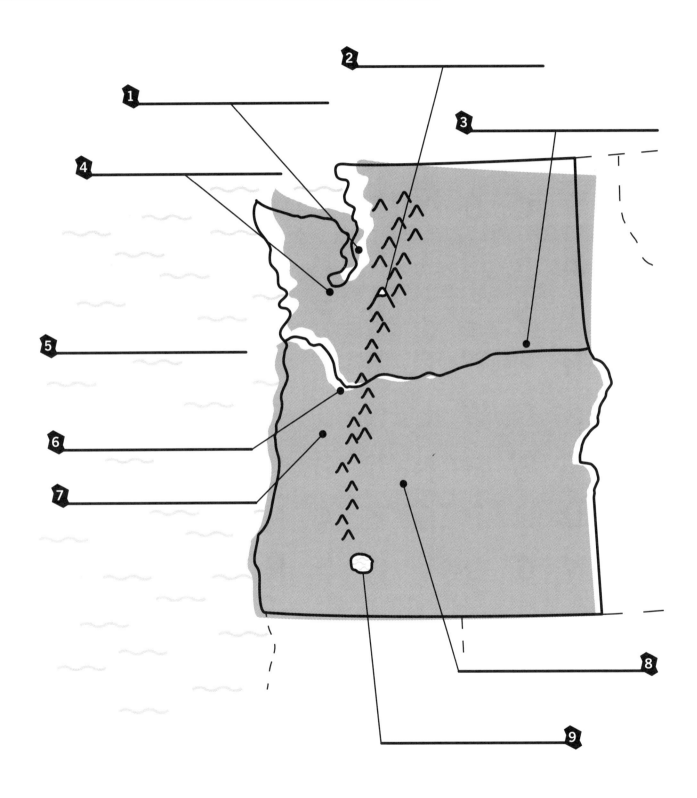

1 _____

2 _____

3 _____

4 _____

5 _____

6 _____

7 _____

8 _____

9 _____

Solution is on page 53.

TOTALLY PACIFIC NORTHWEST!
LOST IN PNW!

```
G H M H F V W L D K F M
R W O T M T R O I B E T
A A C L S T B Y A I L R
N S Q D Y T A T B W G A
D H R M I M H C L E Y I
C I S E T M P E O D L N
O N P W C B Y I L M V I
U G Q W L N A P A E A E
L T W H N D G K K A N R
E O S P O K A N E D O S
E N G O T R O H L R Y B
```

DIABLO LAKE	MT. RAINIER	SPOKANE
GRAND COULEE	MT. ST. HELENS	TACOMA
MT. BAKER	OLYMPIA	WASHINGTON

Solution is on page 54.

LET'S DRAW!

Use the grid to draw the orca.

FOLLOW THE PATH!

Which white water raft makes it past the rocks?

Solution is on page 54.

FIND THE DIFFERENCES!

Can you find all three differences between the two images below?

Solution is on page 55.

CONNECT THE DOTS!

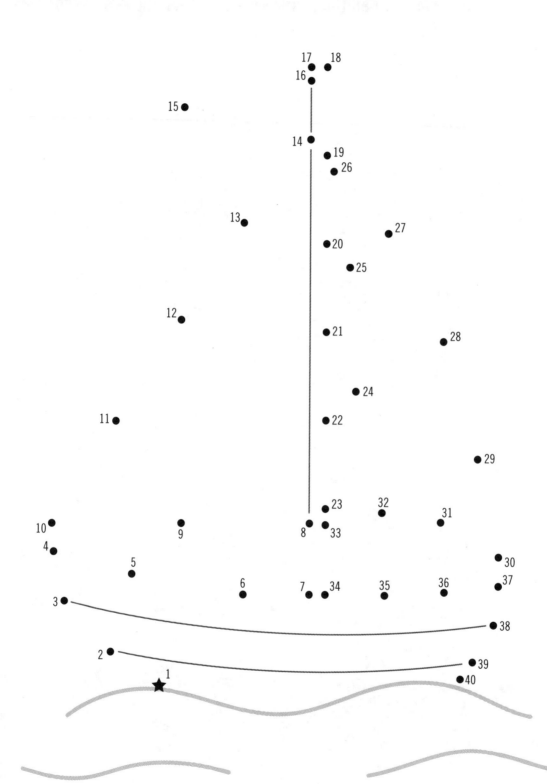

14

LET'S COLOR!

TOTALLY PACIFIC NORTHWEST!
HIDDEN PICTURE!

Use the key to color the shapes below and reveal the hidden picture.

A = Black　　**B = Brown**　　**C = Green**

D = Yellow　　**E = Blue**　　**G = Grey**

Hint!
Color inside the lines!

A PNW DOODLE!

What's crossing the famous Deception Pass Bridge in Washington?

Hint!
A car? A bus? A spaceship? Use your imagination!

TOTALLY PACIFIC NORTHWEST!
CROSSWEIRD PUZZLE!

Use your knowledge of animals and trees found in the **PNW** to solve the puzzle.

◀ ACROSS ▶

3. Mandrone trees are a type of evergreen tree found in the Pacific Northwest, and are known for their red, peeling _____.

4. The sure-footed, woolly white mountain _____ thrives in the Cascade Mountain Range.

6. The great blue _____ can be found foraging for food in coastal areas and wetlands.

8. Trumpeter _____, named for their distinctive call, spend winters in the San Juan Islands, an archipelago in Washington.

DOWN

1. Chinook, coho, and sockeye are all types of _____.

2. Grey _____ are often spotted in Puget Sound in the springtime.

5. This adorable black and white seabird found on the North Pacific coast displays a brightly colored beak during mating season.

7. Black and white _____, also known as killer whales, live in the waters off the coast of the Pacific Northwest.

Solution is on page 55.

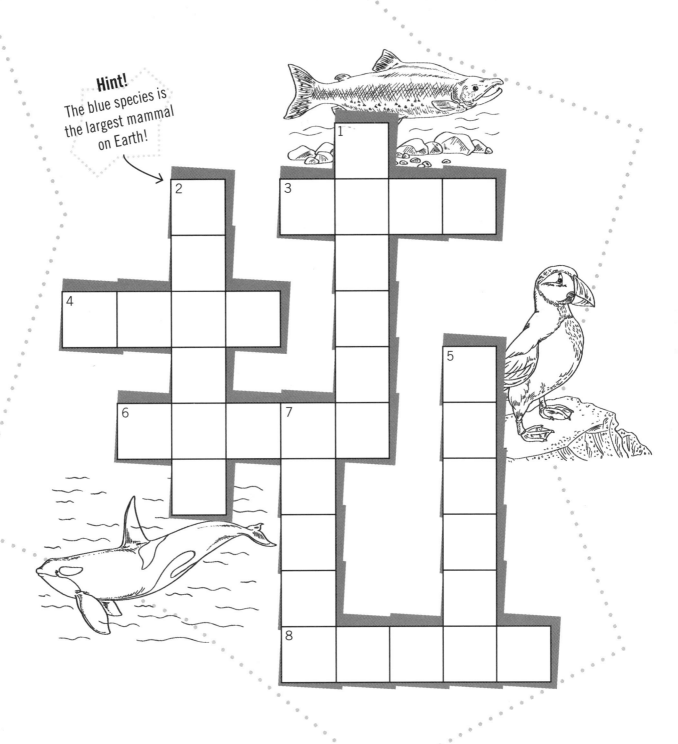

Hint!
The blue species is the largest mammal on Earth!

KEEP PORTLAND WEIRD

TOTALLY PACIFIC NORTHWEST!
TOTALLY SCRAMBLED!

Unscramble the letters of these birds found in the **PNW!**

WOL

ROYPSE

_ _ _ _ _ _

TACMRROON

_ _ _ _ _ _ _ _ _

ALDB GAEEL

_ _ _ _ _ _ _ _ _

FFNUPI

_ _ _ _ _ _

EBUL OHENR

_ _ _ _ _ _ _ _ _

Solution is on page 56.

21

```
T  R  W  Q  U  O  P  M  J  Z  V
W  H  I  T  E  W  A  T  E  R  R
V  A  U  A  P  K  C  O  A  S  T
B  F  I  B  B  V  I  L  B  Z  R
B  I  J  Z  P  O  F  P  N  X  A
F  R  S  I  F  L  I  W  Q  F  I
R  O  B  L  A  C  C  V  M  I  L
J  R  R  D  A  A  D  S  D  E  K
S  T  A  E  V  N  H  J  J  L  U
T  J  Y  I  S  O  D  M  K  B  K
Q  M  O  U  N  T  A  I  N  M  D
```

COAST	MOUNTAIN	TRAIL
FOREST	PACIFIC	VOLCANO
ISLAND	RAIN	WHITEWATER

Solution is on page 56.

MOOSE CROSSING

22

LET'S DRAW!

Use the grid to draw the sailboat.

TOTALLY PACIFIC NORTHWEST!
LET'S SOLVE!

Where does the family go for vacation?

START
HERE!

SEATTLE

CASCADE
MOUNTAIN
RANGE

Solution is on page 56.

A TOTAL SECRET!

Use the key to decode the message.

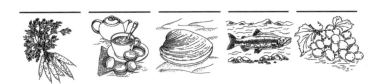

Solution is on page 57.

KEY

= A	= F	= M	= S
= B	= H	= O	= T
= E	= L	= R	

25

TOTALLY PACIFIC NORTHWEST!
LOST IN PNW!

```
Q L D C G I S I Z S I Y B
B A L D M O U N T A I N O
C M K L V C Q I P H P B I
S H O S H O N E F A L L S
N B R Z U D Y G U M D P E
A S S U B N J I C K K C S
K K A I L X V D H T P R T
E I W Q G N C A E G X X A
R A T Z F A M H L P E W T
I R O S B D O O Y L B L E
V P O T A T O M U S E U M
E U T F D L E T K S J Y P
R D H E L L S C A N Y O N
```

BALD MOUNTAIN	IDAHO	SHOSHONE FALLS
BOISE STATE	POTATO MUSEUM	SNAKE RIVER
HELLS CANYON	SAWTOOTH	SUN VALLEY

Solution is on page 57.

A PNW DOODLE!

What's for sale at Pike Place Market?

Hint! Use your imagination!

PUBLIC MARKET CENTER

FARMERS MARKET

WHAT'S IN A NAME?

How many words can you make using letters found in the two words below?

PACIFIC NORTHWEST

Example: PICNIC   WORTH

1. _____

2. _____

3. _____

4. _____

5. _____

6. _____

7. _____

8. _____

9. _____

10. _____

11. _____

12. _____

13. _____

14. _____

15. _____

16. _____

17. _____

18. _____

19. _____

20. _____

Solution is on page 58.

LET'S COLOR!

TOTALLY PACIFIC NORTHWEST!
LOST IN PNW!

```
D L M D T Q B X I Q Y V Z
F K Z R X P O R T L A N D
O V E G E T A R I A N S L
O X O A X J O Y V D B M L
D M B F Y E I T G K G D U
C H I N E S E G A R D E N
A S C A D R P O W E L L S
R P Y L K O V U M J V T H
T H C F O C G A V X K W I
S N L F O R E S T P A R K
M R E Z T A K O J B C T J
U F S B W I S N H P W B Q
S T P N X T C Q D U U O O
```

BICYCLES	DOGS	PORTLAND
BRIDGES	FOOD CARTS	POWELL'S
CHINESE GARDEN	FOREST PARK	VEGETARIANS

Solution is on page 58.

LET'S COLOR!

LET'S MATCH!

Match the correct coastal word with its corresponding image.

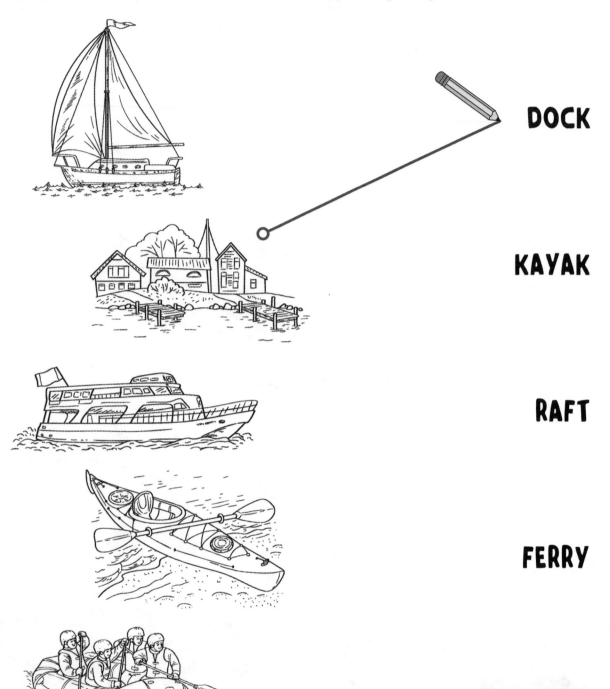

DOCK

KAYAK

RAFT

FERRY

SAILBOAT

Solution is on page 58.

32

A TOTAL SECRET!

Use the key to decode the message.

T H E

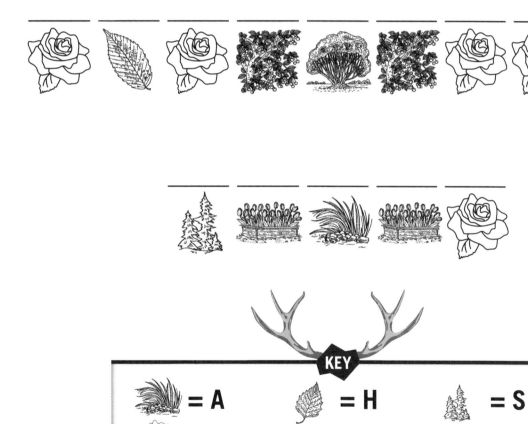

E V E R G R E E N

S T A T E

KEY

= A		= H		= S	
= E		= N		= T	
= G		= R		= V	

Solution is on page 59.

LET'S COLOR!

CROSSWEIRD PUZZLE!

Use your knowledge of popular foods in the **PNW** to solve the puzzle.

◀ ACROSS ▶

1. Pike _____, Seattle's original farmer's market, was established in 1907.

4. Stone fruits like _____ and plums thrive in the damp, cool climate of the Pacific Northwest.

5. The state of _____ is known for its quirky culture, iconic coffee and bookshops, and farm-to-table restaurants.

7. The first _____ opened at Pike Place Market in 1971.

▲ DOWN ▼

1. The state vegetable in Idaho is the _____.

2. Red delicious, fuji, and gala are all types of _____ grown in the state of Washington.

3. The _____ is a giant, edible saltwater clam found deep in the muddy coastal areas of the Pacific Northwest.

6. The Dungeness _____ is a large and tasty shellfish that inhabits Pacific Northwest waters.

Solution is on page 59.

Portland Oregon

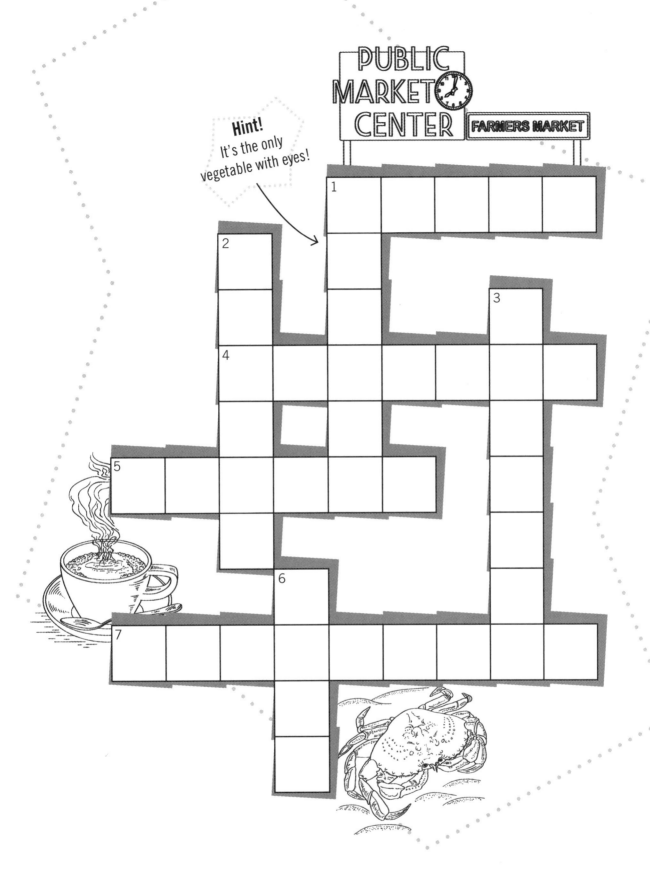

Hint! It's the only vegetable with eyes!

PUBLIC MARKET CENTER FARMERS MARKET

KEEP PORTLAND WEIRD

```
O Y O Q I S G P A H C
E C S R A H I S N I T
R D H H G S A K G N L
Y D I P E A C H E S X
S U S H I L N Z N P M
C C K D K M L I A L A
I F R L P O S F C U T
A R J A C N Q Y I M R
I E M T B C L A M S U
E S L Y K I L U R R H
F H R U F J T T U D O
```

CRAB	ORGANIC	SALMON
CLAMS	PEACHES	SHELLFISH
FRESH	PLUMS	SUSHI

Solution is on page 60.

LET'S COLOR!

TOTALLY PACIFIC NORTHWEST!
LET'S SOLVE!

Help the orca make it to the open ocean.

START
HERE!

Solution is on page 60.

40

FOLLOW THE PATH!

Which puffin finds the Pacific Ocean?

Solution is on page 61.

TOTALLY SCRAMBLED!

Unscramble the letters of these fruits found in the **PNW**.

APSHCEE

— — — — — — —

PRAGES

— — — — — —

RIEHCERS

— — — — — — —

CEUEKIHSRLERB

— — — — — — — — — — — —

RAESP

— — — — —

UMPLS

— — — — —

Solution is on page 61.

MOOSE CROSSING

LET'S DRAW!

Use the grid to draw a Portland rose.

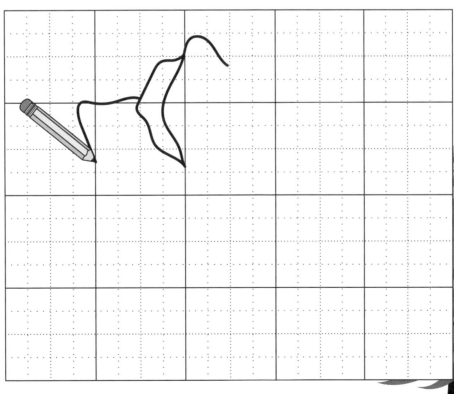

CONNECT THE DOTS!

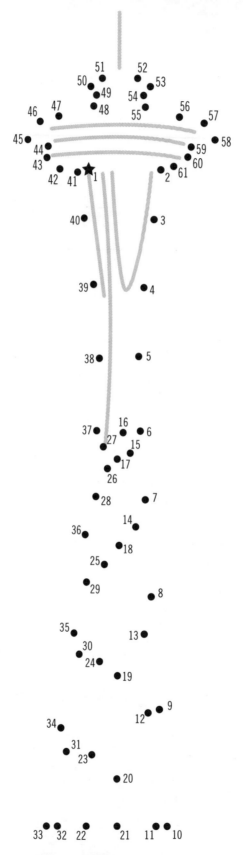

44

TOTALLY PACIFIC NORTHWEST!
LOST IN PNW!

```
J V O E P N V S H B P C L
Q M F W C I K P P A V M V
T A Q W H S O A J L P F B
W R N X I K K C X L T F O
K K O H H F Y E N A B W P
T E V L U G R N X R C L I
M T H C L T P E G D Y N K
L R S X Y A P E M L C N E
U O T H G I C D S O R F P
D I B X L E B L D C N P L
X F Y O A U T E B K G T A
B O O K S T O R E S N E C
M P C Z S E A T T L E T E
```

BALLARD LOCKS	FREMONT	SEATTLE
BOOKSTORES	MARKET	SPACE NEEDLE
CHIHULY GLASS	PIKE PLACE	TROLL

Solution is on page 61.

FIND THE DIFFERENCE!

Can you find all three differences between the two images below?

Solution is on page 62.

CROSSWEIRD PUZZLE!

Use your knowledge of the **PNW** to solve the puzzle.

◀ ACROSS ▶

5. "The _____ City" is one of many nicknames for Seattle.

6. Portland is nicknamed "the city of _____."

8. The Seattle _____ won the *National Football League Super Bowl* Championship in 2014.

▲ DOWN ▼

1. Famous guitarist Jimi _____ was born in Seattle.

2. One of Portland's most famous _____ is Powell's Books.

3. The observation tower that stands out in the Seattle cityscape is called the Space _____.

4. Safeco Field is home to the Seattle _____.

7. The Lewis and _____ expedition spent the winter of 1805-1806 near Astoria, Oregon, resulting in Fort Clatsop.

Solution is on page 62.

MOOSE CROSSING

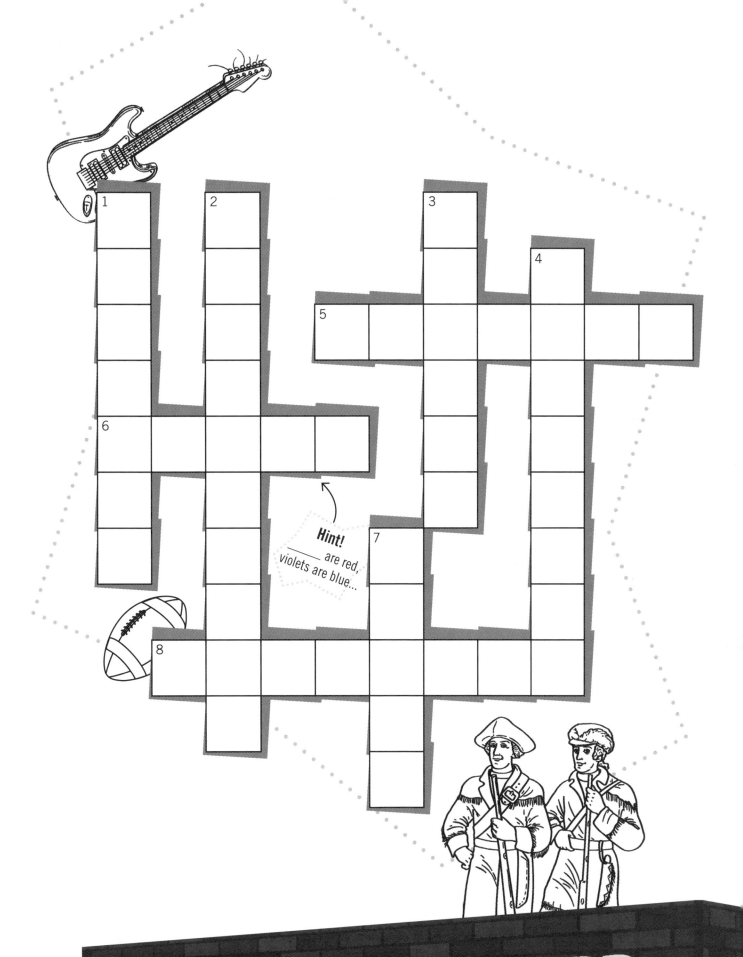

Hint!
_____ are red,
violets are blue...

KEEP PORTLAND WEIRD

A TOTAL SECRET!

Use the key to decode the message.

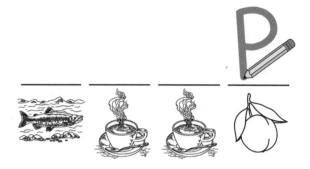

K E E P

P O R T L A N D

W E I R D

KEY

🍦 = A	🐟 = K	🫐 = P			
🌲 = D	🫖 = L	🍔 = R			
☕ = E	🍣 = N	🍇 = T			
🌹 = I	🚴 = O	🕯 = W			

THANKS FOR VISITING THE
PACIFIC NORTHWEST

Solution is on page 62.

SOLUTIONS

Page 2

C L I M B

E V E R Y

M O U N T A I N

Page 3

Page 4

SALMON

ORCA

CRAB

SEAL

SHARK

GREY WHALE

Page 5

Page 7

Page 9

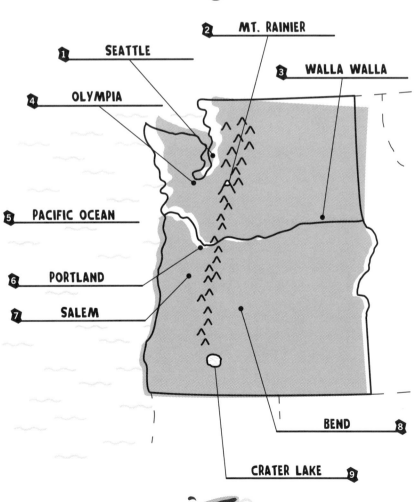

Page 10

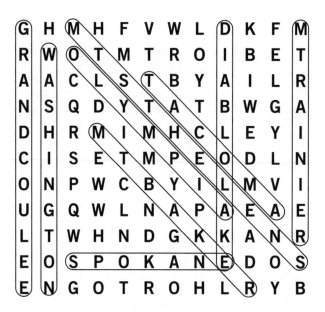

Page 12

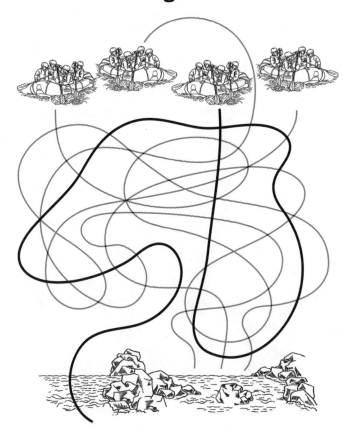

Page 13

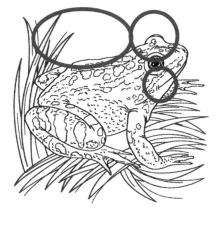

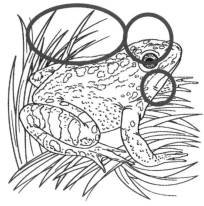

Page 19

Page 20

OWL

OSPREY

CORMORANT

BALD EAGLE

PUFFIN

BLUE HERON

Page 22

```
T R W Q U O P M J Z V
W H I T E W A T E R R R
V A U A P K C O A S T
B F I B B V I L B Z R
B I J Z P O F P N X A
F R S I F L I W Q F I
R O B L A C C V M I L
J R R D A A D S D E K
S T A E V N H J J L U
T J Y I S O D M K B K
Q M O U N T A I N M D
```

Page 24

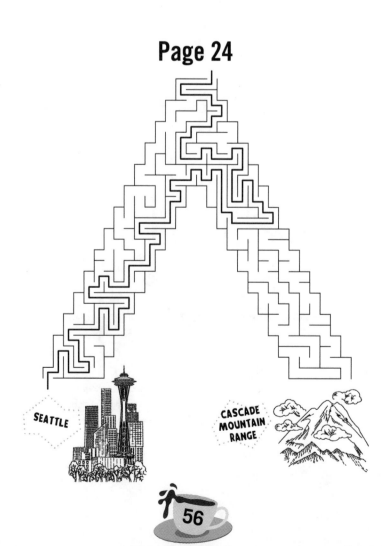

SEATTLE

CASCADE MOUNTAIN RANGE

Page 28

Below are just a few examples of words that could be made with these letters.

PACIFIC NORTHWEST

accept	cow	fan	nice	point	stone
acre	crew	fear	now	raft	toe
ancestor	crop	fern	one	rate	top
apricots	crow	fort	own	ratio	town
apron	ear	fraction	parent	reaction	two
awe	earn	infect	part	scenario	wasp
can	east	inspector	pat	sent	wet
canister	eat	nap	paw	snap	worn
corn	factor	new	pen	software	wrap

Page 30

Page 32

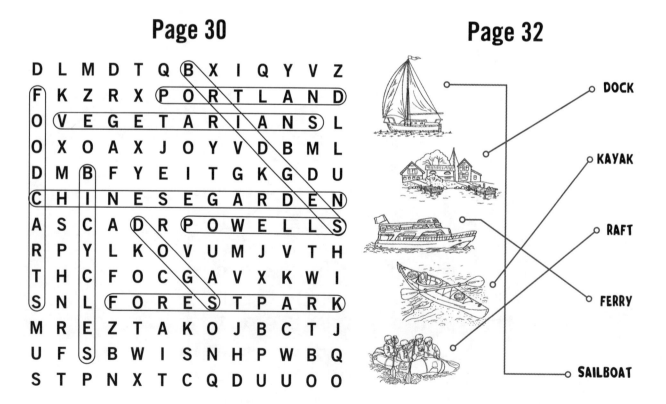

Page 33

T H E

E V E R G R E E N

S T A T E

Page 37

```
              ¹P L A C E
       ²A      O
        P      T       ³G
       ⁴P E A C H E S
        L      T       O
    ⁵O R E G O N       D
        E              U
        S     ⁶C       C
   ⁷S T A R B U C K S
              R        K
              A
              B
```

Page 38

```
O Y O Q I S G P A H C
E C S R A H I S N I T
R D H H G S A K G N L
Y D I P E A C H E S X
S U S H I L N Z N P M
C C K D K M L I A L A
I F R L P O S F C U T
A R J A C N Q Y I M R
I E M T B C L A M S U
E S L Y K I L U R R H
F H R U F J T T U D O
```

Page 40

Page 41

Page 42

 PEACHES

GRAPES

 CHERRIES

HUCKLEBERRIES

 PEARS

PLUMS

Page 46

Page 47

Page 49

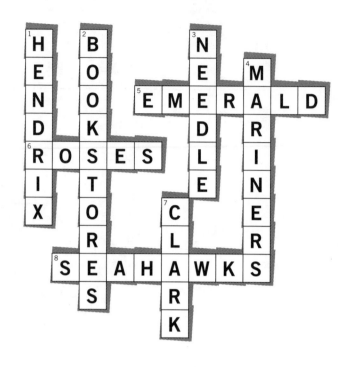

Page 50

K E E P

P O R T L A N D

W E I R D